WITH NO HAT

Also By
Tim Seibles

Body Moves

Hurdy-Gurdy

Hammerlock

Buffalo Head Solos

Fast Animal

One Turn Around The Sun

Kerosene (chapbook)

Ten Miles An Hour (chapbook)

Voodoo Libretto: New & Selected Poems

WITH NO HAT

Tim Seibles

Etruscan Press

Etruscan Press
Wilkes University
84 West South Street
Wilkes-Barre, PA 18766
(570) 408-4546

www.etruscanpress.org

Published 2026 by Etruscan Press
Printed in the United States of America
Cover design by Lisa Reynolds
Cover image by Jennifer Fish
Interior design and typesetting by Muhammad Imran
The text of this book is set in Adobe Jenson Pro.

First Edition

17 18 19 20 5 4 3 2 1

Library of Congress Cataloguing-in-Publication Data

Names: Seibles, Tim author
Title: With no hat / Tim Seibles.
Description: First Edition. | Wilkes Barre : Etruscan Press, 2026. |
Summary: "Celebrating his 70th year, Tim Seibles presents With No Hat, a new collection with a long history. Energized and original, With No Hat also offers a retrospective of Seibles' life and career-including his signature sassy villanelles; pop up cameos of cartoon characters; meditations on aging, death, identity, and at-one-ment with all beings; and leading the parade-the main character: the poem itself-lithe and mischievous-not only bareheaded, but in the full glory of his birthday suit. Yeats says, "I made my song a coat...but there's more enterprise in walking naked." With No Hat enterprises-strides, sprints, gavottes, and tiptoes through a life work of forging imagination into unforgettable tableaus, spanning self and other, and embracing and assessing, with Seibles' empathic but cold eye, our culture and our lives in mortal crisis"-- Provided by publisher.
Identifiers: LCCN 2025048718 | ISBN 9798990767843 paperback
Subjects: LCSH: Autobiographical poetry, American | LCGFT: Poetry
Classification: LCC PS3569.E475 W58 2026
LC record available at https://lccn.loc.gov/2025048718

Please turn to the back of this book for a list of the sustaining funders of Etruscan Press.

This book is printed on recycled, acid-free paper.

*In remembrance of Danny Solis, Thomas Sayers Ellis,
and Baron Wormser*

One'a these days
I got to be free.

--Jimi Hendrix
"Hear My Train A'Comin"

TABLE OF CONTENTS

ACT III

ACT IV

ACKNOWLEDGEMENTS

Some of these poems have appeared previously in the following magazines:

Beloit Poetry Journal
Dalhousie Review
*En*Trance*
Erato
The Fight & The Fiddle
Huizache
James Dickey Review
Nimrod International Journal
Obsidian Literature & Arts in the African Diaspora
Only Poems
Pangyrus
Ploughshares
Poem-a-Day
Rattle
Shenandoah
The Southampton Review
The New Guard

Anthologies:

Signed, Sealed, Delivered
The Seven Cities
What Saves Us
Why I Wrote This Poem

RIDDLE ME THIS

Who made the lock,
the door, the cage?

Who hid the key?

Are you what you
think you are

or what *they* say
you seem to be?

Is the fire cold
inside you?

Since when
and how   and *why?*

When you lived
as you chose

did you choose
or did you only

seem to be?

Who made the cage,
the lock, the door?

Who has the key?

ACT I

WITH NO HAT,

no shirt, no pants, the poem walks
the early afternoon. Summer sun
spots the odd shape on the road
and offers a cloud for shade.

The poem is headed downtown
with its revelations, its beauty, all
the intricate parts, finally
open to the general public

who, though they try to deny it,
have always wanted to see
beneath the vintage clothes.
The poem's previous modesty

and stealth, its humility and
restraint, its patient, soft-spoken
invitations have served no one really—
not even the poem itself, which has
always wanted the spotlight:

the red carpet, the sequined gown,
the top hat, velvet lapels, ruby
slippers, all its big, front teeth
inlaid with gold. The first people
the poem passes look   look away

look again: their hope swelling
like a fresh bump on the head.
One man tries *9-1-1*, but the 9
skips then shimmies like a new

disciple, and the brotha's big 'fro
bursts into cotton candy. The poem
loves it, loves being out, being *seen*—
the almost-cool walk flips

to a Denzel stroll: *I'm kickin*
new flava   in ya ear, it says unquietly
meeting the eyes of drivers who swerve,
so sure they see what must be

a mirage: this buck-naked angel
rump-shakin beside the witless
sprawl of their lives, their heads
anointed with apocryphal music.
The cars refuse the road—

their horns reborn scatting
a fanfare of *Funkadelic* clarinets.
This is my body, the poem says.
Take and eat.

*Craig Mack wrote the hip-hop anthem "Flava in Ya Ear."

LITTLE STAR BLUES VILLANELLE

Someday no one will wonder where you are
Your name won't be on anyone's mind
Remember "Twinkle, Twinkle, Little Star"?

Count up the hours you scratched in your car
Where were you going most of the time?
Someday no one will wonder where you are—

Maybe you think I take things too far
I think it was mom who taught me to rhyme
She sang *Twinkle, Twinkle, Little Star*

Some days die like big bugs in the tar
Who was that small boy at the start of your mind?
Someday your mother won't know who you are

Woulda been nice to be crowned the czar
Tell everyone else what to do all the time:
You betta Twinkle, Twinkle, Little Star!

Whatchu think makes people work so hard?
Like money's some mountain we s'posed to climb
One day no one will wonder how you are

Mostly what kills me won't leave any scar
I bet I know why most people go blind
They need "Twinkle, Twinkle, Little Star"

Let's sit in the shade by that tree in the yard
And chew on the hours with their lemony rind

Someday no one will wonder what you are
Remember "Twinkle, Twinkle, Little Star"

ANTS

Midsummer you'll see one
far from the yard, maybe
in a bookstore, third floor
of the mall—or somehow
whipping across town
with you in the car.

There it is: stepping along
the dusty dashboard,
antennae askew, six tiny feet
marking a straight line
pausing once twice as if trying
to remember a missed turn

but without panic, though
it's probably hungry
and a little pissed—
desperate for the lean
chemical trail of its colony kin

who by now are a million
ant miles away, just beginning
to notice that *you-know-who*
hasn't been seen for a while.
Maybe their feelers twitch
with grief or a little envy.

Saw one today
on the basketball court
and wished I could believe
what that ant believed
with those fancy sneaks
flashing all around.

Years ago, in Philadelphia—
Sharpnack Street: row houses
block after block, paint peeling
on the porches, one faded address
after another—I was looking
for Donna's.

She had the biggest afro
in the city and a smile
like a lead singer
taking the mike: Donna Keene,
the girl I called a "tackhead"
back in 7th grade because
no one had told me
what puberty could do.

I must've had the street wrong
and soon found myself deep
in the turf held by *The Clang*:
tough guys mostly my age
and always ready to *move*
on a stranger   and I knew

those dudes didn't know me.
But I just kept on
while the dark flickered
with the streetlights
starting to buzz and the city
like a black leather jacket.

I was sixteen, out
of the house with nobody
bossing me around, lost
in a night that never
seemed to notice.

It was like that today—
me, wandering a neighborhood
that should've been familiar,
looking for someone
I like, but really

nothing is familiar:
not these pocked streets
and half-trimmed hedges,
not my own busy head
stocking up on fear,

not even my country
though I was born here
almost 70 years ago, but what
can you do? What can anybody

actually do   but keep on walking

TURN IT UP

Brothaz in gangs, man, they don' see no other way.
--Jeff Bryant

Hey, DJ—bring that back
--Ludacris

Days when I think we might
live forever: sunlight on the corner,
cool brims every color,

one 'a y'all singin some Al Green.
A nice breeze: one leaf, then another,
the whole tree dancing.

What I want to say
is this: we do not have
to die—we do *not*

have to die
with our eyes broken
and blood burning our fists.

Brothaz,
today is a door,
the hour, still open.

Though the trap has been set,
though the graves

keep calling, we do not
have to listen.

Look.

After all these years, Time
still lives "down around the way"

waiting for all'a y'all
to come over: the plates are hot,
the bass is bangin—the DJ
sayin, *And ya don't stop.*

Unlock your soul.
Turn up your heart.

NAÏVE

I love you but I don't know you
--Mennonite Woman

When I was seven, I walked home
with Dereck DeLarge, my arm

slung over his skinny shoulders,
after-school sun buffing our lunch boxes.

So easy, that gesture, so light—
the kind of love that lands like a leaf.

It was 1963.
We were two black boys

whose snaggle-toothed grins
held a thousand giggles.

Remember? Remember
wanting to play

every minute, as if *that*
was why we were born?

Those hands that bring us
shouting into this life

must open like a fanfare
of big band horns.

Though this world is nothing
like where we'd been,

we come anyway, astonished—

as if to Mardi Gras in full swing.
There must be a time

when a child's heart builds
a chocolate sunflower

while katydids burnish the day
with their busy wings.

This itching fury that
holds me now—this knowing

the early welcome
that once lived inside me

was somehow sent away:
how I talk myself back

into all the regular disguises
but still walk these streets

believing in the weather
of the unruined heart.

My friends, with crow's feet
edging their eyes,

keep looking for a kinder
city, though they don't

want to seem naïve.
When was the last time

you wrapped your arm
around someone's shoulder

and walked him home?

GAME DAY

for Colin Kaepernick

Here they come: Bobbleheads.
Hot dogs. Big dudes and beer.

The stadium, a living thing.
Little kids fizz like fresh *Pepsi*.

You always loved the game.
Didn't you always get picked first

in the schoolyard—like stepping
into a good dream: the ball

in your hands, you were a snake
with wings—a shimmy, a shake

and the defense disappeared.

Then came your faith
in highlights—catch,

cutback, touchdown, blood.

The stars pointing up
to a God they knew kept score

and the cheerleaders: sequins
in their eyes, smiles you hoped

meant something sexual. The TV
sizzled   and the players

on your posters promised
someday you might never be alone:

crossing a street, cruising the mall,
your face, the big surprise—your long run

the ESPN on everyone's lips.
You had to believe

a bright jersey and a good arm
could change everything,

even your tough country.

And weren't they wonderful,
those days when you knew nothing

could catch you—*runnin*
like he was late for the last bus!—

and maybe what gave you that
sidestep, that blind speed

was partly fear: The Past

re-set, always scheming
to chase you down.

But wasn't the NFL *The Emerald City*?

Weren't you the flying house
for a while? Weren't you

Dorothy? Weren't you

the Scarecrow
and the Wizard of Oz?

Hard to believe
that History is no dream.

The stadium rings, even now,
like a medieval cathedral:

the anthem fades, the uneasy
citizens take their seats.

These days, you watch it all
on TV. You remember

bright mustard, fresh
meat boosting the breeze—

and when one team starts to lose,
the shouts, the jeers replay

some old questions: *who's bleeding*
on the field? Who's howling

from the stands? How simply
this long season continues—

like a kind of obedience,
a bone bruise that lingers

or some other thing
not mentioned in the song:

AND YET,

the poem remains
unafraid: a black Pegasus
tattooed on its
bare chest.

Do whatever you want!
the poem taunts, as people
steady the scaffold
and test the noose.

It's dawn.
The poem's been
awake for hours
wondering why

it has to be
this way, when once
there was song
and so much promise.

Do your worst,
the poem laughs, flexing
its pecs so the black wings
flap and the poem

begins to rise, begins
to see itself
far above the mob,
beyond all the madness—

objective, detached—
like a coffee shop:
citizens coming in

with no dirty looks,
no axes to grind,

just wanting to meet
the endless workday

with a ten-cylinder heart.
Just get your coffee

and get out! the poem shouts—

the sun in full fury now,
elbowing the clouds.

TWIN

A few hours ago, a man
some call *mentally*
challenged told me
about his pulled tooth.

"Still hurts bad,"
he said. People walked by,
their shadows cursive
in the late sun.

This man—white,
maybe forty—spoke
as though he *knew* me,
knew I would know
how to stop the pain.

I'd seen him around—
unsure in the crosswalk,
sipping free cocoa
at the coffee shop—
said hello a couple times.

His eyes held that
first ache, that hope
we hold before time
hardens our faces

and I understood
for a moment—my life
and his: what it means

to suffer quietly on Earth,
confused by the way
things are—having

no idea, really,
what to do
or who to ask.

THREE STOOGES BLUES VILLANELLE

You know   I don' wanna know what I know
Most days I'd rather think like a child
I got this gray beard, but that's only for show

When I was little, I was happy to grow
But after I stopped, they put me on trial
I really don' wanna know   what I know

'Member them days tryin'a shape up your 'fro
And hopin "the honeys" would fall for your smile?
Most of'em knew it was only for show

Few days from now, this'll be long ago
And I prolly won't feel like this afta'while
I'll still have my beard but mostly for show

Brothaz walk around takin blow after blow
Who doesn't dream of a green desert isle?
Gotta find a way not to know what you know

I wanna get free, but the world says *No*
You live long enough: you get used to denial
My beard is free, but that's just for show

Can't hang your head all the time, although
Like Gil said, it's been winter for a while
Wish I didn't have ta know what I know

Remember *The Stooges*—Shemp, Curly, and Moe?
I sat on the floor and just laughed like a child

I really don't like that I   know what I know
So, I act all grown up, but it's only for show

*Gil Scott-Heron wrote the song "Winter In America."

RIDDLE

from what we cannot hold
the stars are made
--WS Merwin

When I saw the forest
it was late afternoon.

The sky held the color
of something
almost forgotten.
I pulled off the road—
found a gravel path
sloping toward the trees.

It had to be the light
that remembered
my last Saturday at Y camp:
freshly husked corn
roasting on the cob
and all the nervous cicadas
calming down for dark.

Because I didn't know
the handle could be hot
I burned myself
pulling a skillet from the fire
and was cursing quietly
when a blonde boy
I hadn't met
told me to put my fingers
in his milk. *It's okay,*
he said, *won't hurt as much.*

I was 12, stuck on the step
between childhood and puberty
just starting to understand
that I liked being alone
and trying the riddle
of how to be a person
who might turn
into an "adult."

At the time, I did not
have these words
but on this drive
I'd been wondering
about what I'd become
and how I live in this country.

It all came back:
the red and white carton
with a bent straw in it
my fingers starting to blister
then the white kid's
shy shrug of a smile.

In the forest
it was already night.

EITHER WAY

for Cornelius Eady

Days when something grazes my shoulder.

Sunlight, sidewalk, the shadows sharp.

The sky holds a cold, unbreakable blue
that says *Why look   up here?*

*

Doesn't seem like so far back: couldn't dance,
scared of girls, I heard Smokey sing

goin to a go-go   with that soft crystal in his voice.
Pictures, music caught somewhere inside me—

I'm sick of memory:

my younger self, still here,
wanting a way out of this

who I am now: this bizzy-all-the-time,
this—this itch middle of my back.

*

But who was that kid in the basement?—

all alone with The Miracles
moving his feet. The orange couch

covered in plastic, black marks
on the beige linoleum.

*

Something about solitude—if you can stand it—
makes you feel wise: the voice

in your head   talking its way somewhere,

pressing you to believe
what it says

and, though you can't remember when,
you grow into it

or you don't: each thought breaks
into the next—keeps on, turns back.

Either way, you don't ever
really   under

*

stand. Just as you get used to the snow
shingling your hair, The Temptations, one

by one, begin to leave. *My girl,*
my girl fills the coffee shop

and gently bobs your head.
What is it

*

that your life
forgot to mention?

Hum a few bars you say.

ACT II

AFTER GETTING

Jack Daniels and *Wrangler*
as sponsors, the poem has begun

a career in professional
bull riding—

something it has often
threatened to do—but now,

having already been bounced
on its big head by *Wham-Bam*

Thank You, Ma'am—and presently,
gloved and strapped to *Sweet Bruiser,*

the poem wonders aloud
if it has overplayed

the macho thing, perhaps

*under*imagined the mercilessness
of the not-so-contemplative world.

"Don't think so much," the rodeo clowns
grin and shake their heads

as if to warn and affirm at the same time.
Hearing the giddy, half-tipsy

rustle and buck
of the country-western crowd,

the poem wishes it were also hooting
and hefting a foamy brew

and not feeling *Sweet Bruiser's* back
quake beneath its

chafed buns and blue leather chaps.
Still, the poem is proud

of its rough and tumble ways, proud
of not backing down, daring

to do something no one expects.
"Ready," the official asks, one hand on the gate.

The poem checks its grip, then nods,
playing extra cool while its heart sweats.

BLACKFACE

It's not that you are
not   pretty tired of talking

about *race* and/or *racism* or what
ever someone wants to call the

various configurations of
lunacy related to the-

to the mistreatment
of a person or persons

based on face,

hair texture, and
other related

etceteras. You are- you
really are. It's just that

today   some photos-
photos have emerged:

emerged   as if on their own,
by their own power, as if

the Governor of Virginia had
popped up like a dandelion

on an otherwise
nice looking lawn—

that you had admired and now
would rather forget about or

aggressively ignore or pretend
not to

notice, which is some
thing that you- that you've almost

perfected—like, for example,
when you're sitting in a

coffee shop and bad
music comes on

and the song tries
to bore into your brain

like a botfly
larva. You don't allow

that: you fend it off,
I mean- I mean you

give it a good shove
away from your ears, *out of*

earshot as they say,
so you can go on—

like right now, there's
TV news in the room:

more news that you can
not tolerate, refuse to abide,

can't stand, will not stand

for. You just want
to build your life

around a latte
this morning and

sip your way out
of the situation, tamp down

the noise without getting up
set- without feeling set

up   by the media,
as though they knew

you'd be watching, as if
all of this had been

planned, had been cast,
so a whole *live*

audience could see
how you'd react,

as though you're-
you're some kind of

patient but
probably going to be O

K.

SOMETIMES FREDDY BLUES VILLANELLE

for Freddy Porter

Sometimes Freddy would talk to the trees
And the brothaz would just laugh half the time
But a few of'em said *Have mercy on me*

Think about all that good sunlight you see
Yet somehow the days peel away like rind
Mostly Freddy just talked to the trees

Branches say somethin when they shake in the breeze
Believe what'chu want, but it could be a sign
Maybe they're sayin *Have mercy on me*

Sundays I sit with a brain full'a fleas
And listen to people speak for the Divine
Wish they would go and just talk to the trees

Hiding a scream is like holdin a sneeze
It's all you can do not to lose your damn mind
I see why people say *Have mercy on me*

I'm starting to list like a ship in rough seas
I guess you just have to laugh half the time
And think about Freddy and walk with the trees

I look at my watch, but my watch is a tease
Or maybe it's always a quarter past nine
Them thin little hands have mercy on me

Think about SpongeBob with his home in the sea
Wouldn't you visit if you had the time?

Sometimes Freddy would talk to the trees
You can see why I say *Mercy, mercy on me*

MAGA HAT: The Storm

What they *can't* see
is the faith
we have in the past.
The Confederacy
never died. You think
ghosts are making
all these flags?
Call me a good ol' boy,
call me a racist, but
don't call me too late
to *Stop The Steal!*

The liberal dribble says
we breached the Capitol,
attacked *democracy*,
but how can that
be true? It ain't democracy
if you don't win
and without a President
who really knows you

what does freedom
mean? And honestagod,
could there really
be 81 million Americans
that don't love a billionaire
who's ready to smack
the lefty media
in its lib-tard mouth?

I mean, he's a genius—
he said so himself. Q knows

we gotta save our country.
"Stand back and stand by!"

I mean, who else has the guts?

HOLDEN CAULFIELD: SECRET IDENTITY, 1951

Nobody knew I was colored. At Pencey Prep
I mean. Nobody knew. Seriously, my hair—
which my mother called muddy-blonde—
was almost straight. It really was.
And when that hard curl started creeping
I'd cut it quick so there'd be no hint
of the negro in me.

It wasn't that *I* minded being half and half.
I didn't. Not at all—I mean, colored people
make music a thousand times more danceable.
My pop, a corny white guy, is always trying
to play the blues. Such a phony: bobbing
his head, praying over the keys like he's
Pinetop Perkins or something, but

he's such a racist. He really is. The reason
he wouldn't marry my mother, see
the reason was: he didn't want to live
"in some colored neighborhood." He wanted
"respectable society". Such an ass.
You can't believe people sometimes.
You really can't. Even if you're related,
they can be pretty damn disappointing.

And Pencey, of course, at Pencey
I kept pretty quiet. Of course, I woulda
got thrown out if anybody got wind of me
being half-Negro, but if you really looked—
at my lips, I mean   and my nose—
you could tell something was going on
with my *heritage*.

Once I brought up Billie Holiday and
Count Basie   and this kid (I think it was
Ackley) said, "What's with the jungle music—
some nigger in your woodshed?"
I almost punched him in the mouth,
but I'm such a coward. I just walked away
whistling "Strange Fruit" really loud.

My whole life was make-believe.
Goddam private schools. I wanted to say
I *am* a Negro, you dumbass,
but I never did. I swear my whole life
has been hide and seek. Such a lie!
Passing. For white, I mean. Really
insane: the whole race thing.

Even going to church every Sunday:
all the "love thy neighbor" crap.
They're all smiley-faced, hand-shakin',
half-ass phonies. And me too—and
maybe the whole country. *God bless
this, that, and the other.* And look:
us colored folks get hell kicked out of us!
That's why I'm an atheist. I really am.

So, I don't have many friends—
except maybe my kid sister, Phoebe.
She kills me. She tells people
she's colored all the time,
but nobody believes her. That's the thing
about people. They never believe you.
They really don't. And nobody thinks
about anything. Even if you ask'em
a pretty general question—like *Why?
Why any of this?* They won't answer.
They won't even try.

FED UP WITH

the rattrap of gender,
the *he*-or-*she* thing everywhere

like an endless outbreak
of the flu, the poem shaves

her head, waxes his
underarms, throws away *their*

brassiere, and saunters
onto the boardwalk with one leg

conspicuously hirsute. They care
and do *not* care when people

suck teeth and leer
at the sky-blue eyeshadow,

black Fu Manchu, tiny
come-hither shorts and

scuffed-up, oxblood work boots.
Eat your heart out, the poem sneers,

hands on hips, knowing
anatomy is an accident

of birth, the self a riddle, both
to itself and to the many others

handcuffed to *he*-or-*she-ism*
as if to a litter of whimpering

mice-pups. One muscular brotha
tries to understand. "Is this

freedom?" he asks, side-eyeing
the poem's high-flown

sashay. Most days, this dude
was glad to be a man

but, like a werewolf at full moon,
the macho madness of it all

suddenly shows itself: the chronic
worry about *The Johnson,*

the required *cool,*
so much tough talk…

These balls
will never pronounce

my one true name!
the poem scoffs,

blowing him a kiss,
combing their curly 'fro:

unable to see this life

as metaphor
but completely unafraid

of all it seemed to seem.

IAGO, UNFETTERED

I'm no green
monster: I've shared
my share of sweat-
damp sheets—and with maidens
deadly more fair
than Desdemona, I dare say.

What *is* romance? A two-faced
beast, each saying always
what the other
misunderstands. Such fuss
finds web for silly flies.
Tis trouble

that I love, its inscrutable
stealth: the way it
appears from nowhere
and gains all
attention—like a virgin
birth or a new ghost
who spurs your head
till you give up the lease
and go.

Comfort comes in believing
men could not be cruel
but for ignorance
of kinder ways: *Romance*
indeed! Yet the lack

of such faith cuts and bleeds
unbearable days, while
an abundance of it threads
mischief into lovely lives: lo,
I did not do what I did
for meanness sake. Othello,

don't claw your face. Regret
is a legless steed. I confess
I found you marvelous: a heart
more stout than most—
with a head to match—but

such a riddle   then
what mortal fun: to build
a weather brash, black
enough to blow you down
and snuff love's lamp
in the same now.

To see it done   and *live,*
to hear that sharp
consumptive cry. O, more
than this, I could not hope
to ask.

ISLAND OF SALT CAY, July 2024

"The salt companies left in '69."
--Maurice

Mr. Poli's still here, 92—
thin as a heron's leg, and *Miz* Nettie
baking big breads, bright white hair
like moonlight above her brown face,

and Willie from Haiti, tending his tiny bar,
and Eloisa who opens her place
with a laugh. Nobody's rich,
but nobody seems poor.

On Salt Cay, History walks
with a bold nonchalance: the salinas
muddy from neglect, the forty-some black folks:
children of the children of Africans
bought to rake and carry this flavor
for the world, business buildings abandoned now,
gaunt, ready for collapse, and white people
mostly gone but for blue-eyed Beatrix and a British couple—
old Europe drifting like steam from their tea.

But the beaches blaze egret-white, and the sea
beats a bachata on the rocks—sings, *Sunlight*
moves with me! More donkeys than people,
forgotten houses muffled in dust, rock-strewn
dirt roads, the subtle hens clucking
the underbrush, ants everywhere
paving thin lanes to their hidden cities.

I'm an American, Black and full of America
so, it's hard to say where I belong, but I would
come back to say *Yes* to Salt Cay and the chance
to forget that: yes, to the wary lizards and the donkeys
whose deep, sleepy eyes dream yes to fresh water
and stalky greens to eat.

And, of course, yes, to the ocean—
so many shoals of blue, so many cool flames
of impossibly ebullient blue, and the grasses
walking with the wind, the bumblebees
forever revving their wings, the night rains,
the thorny acacias, and always,
always a little salt on your skin.

LAST BLACK CARGO BLUES VILLANELLE

Can't unnerstand how we fit in dis scene
The day fall down like a man wit no bones
Don't look like dis the dream I tried ta dream

Not sure what make dem white eyes so mean
Spent most'a my life tryin not ta cry alone
Can't hardly see how I fit in dis scene

Pockets so empty even springtime ain't green
Look like my best chance went off on its own
'Cause dis ain't the dream I been tryin'a dream

I bet dis the saddest place I ever seen
Me and my heart prolly destined ta roam
How'd I get caught in dis hard-time scheme?

Guess some hammer done fell on my dream
You know how it go when your good luck get gone
Who want dis place ta be like it be?

You hear what I say   but dat ain't what I mean
Been grindin so long my song scrape like a moan
Gotta get myself outta dis scheme

They say when I die leas' my soul be clean
Maybe they think dis old head turnt ta stone
'Cause *dat* ain't the dream I been tryin'a dream

Dis country roll on like a floodwater stream
Nothin much left'a my body but bone

Look like I'm fit'n'ta die in dis scene
But sher ain't the way it was s'posed ta be

Note: Zora Neale Hurston's recently recovered book, *Barracoon,* features a series of interviews with Cudjo Lewis (born Oluale Kossola in West Africa) in which he describes his life before and after being captured and shipped to the American South to be enslaved. He was one of the few who remained alive in the 1920s.

RIDDLE 2

It was already evening
after six: August—

the sun, bright as anger
drove me to look for shade

and there was a mountain
not too far away:

it would be cooler there
with so many trees

and the sleepy animals
settling in the shadows—

someone said there was
a clear pond partway up

where you could splash your face
and suddenly see why

things are the way they are
so I walked and I wondered

what such knowing might do:
would I stop being afraid

of what could happen and
what might happen after that?

Would I stop asking questions
about *systems*, gnashing my teeth

on the ideas that have built
this world, *this* kind of world—

and the walk had gotten long
but I was getting there, though now

the sun was gone, taking with it
the burnt-orange hem of the sky

and with the risen dark
the mountain disappeared

THE POEM HAD STARTED TO BELIEVE

Welcome to The Revolution, cabrón…
--Danny Solis

that what's wrong with the world
cannot be fixed, will not be stopped,
no matter what the poem proposes,
no matter how hard the poem sweats:

the sky swims with crocodiles,
every day the daylight shrinks
like a cheap shirt. *Nothing fits,*
the poem mutters. *I do Not*

fit in this world. Imagine
an octopus in a tank top,
a brontosaurus in skinny jeans,
the poem's brain—a firestorm
crammed into a snow globe:

I came here for grasshoppers,
for gingerbread and the mellow smell of cedar,
for love with all its soulful incantations,
for poetry: preemptive, impolite, polyphonic—
and for kisses: latent, lavish, salacious,
kisses   long as an opera.

But what do I get?
Chronic stupidity, bad religions
and bigotry by the boatload,
half the world worked to death,
the other half hungry,
politicians bouncing on the laps
of lobbyists, while the rich
try to stifle their giggles.

I have put up and put up
and put up with it, the poem spits,
smacking its head, hair nappy
and matted, its fingernails cracked.

The poem had studied
the rules: applied for better
verbs, maintained its soft growl
of restrained aggravation,
that spritz of semi-ecstatic wonder,
but now it knows   it's just
a minstrel show, a silly soft shoe,
jazz hands, obsequious and degrading.

They treat us like fluff,
the poem sneers, *like*
the dandruff of the headless.
What's with all this backbiting
about big time publication?

I remember my first lines—
the sharp tang of truth on my tongue,
the shuffle of days
before they were named.
Who hog-tied me to these pages?

I am the child of pagans
and poltergeists, of Zulus
and the Comanche—I am
the soul's paella, all the moans
of every Friday night.

You, who have paved
this stolen land, played
this broken story, poured
this comfy quicksand for the heart,
beware:

I was not born to make peace
with you—or for your sake.

It's time the people knew,
time The Spirit scrambled,
for the wind to remember,
and the fists to sing.

I dream with red ants and wolves,
with clownfish and corn snakes.
I am better weather and bright wings—
for Gaza, for Southside Chicago,
Cheyenne River, and the Sahel.

As prophesied by no one
I have risen again:
like a welt after the lash,
like a dandelion
from the forehead of a cyclops,
like a horde of locusts
after the field is bare.

Go   tell it

ACT III

MOVIE

It was already on when you came in:

a two-lane road, the car's high beams
blaming the dark. In the rearview mirror,
the downtown of a city—familiar, but not.

Because you have found yourself
cast in the world without your consent,

you think you must be something
like other people—like the dude
two rows back with his face lit by a phone

or maybe like the star   behind the wheel:
one eye swollen, the other tight in a squint.

You want to know what happened,
what's happening and where the road
will go and when and soon

she's standing outside a *7-11*
filling up her dusty, dark-blue Mustang.

Early sun steams the back window.
Maybe she drove all night—

her voice: part sorrow, part wind
under the overhang. *Why didn't I*

see it before, she asks aloud
for everyone, flexing the engine,

ready to go.
This is the story of what

happens when what
has seemed one way

turns out to be *another* way
like a priest.

Even when the day is sprung,
and you wake up trapped

in everything, you want this face
on screen: cool, without a flinch.

Even the way she steers
is a declaration—you want to drive

like that.
You could drive like that:

like somebody in charge,
somebody who "knows the deal."

On the passenger seat,
half-stashed in her scarf, a .38.

Your mind moves to revenge: how

your circumstances   just don't
make any sense. You want

to know who made it this way

and one chance to make them
back down and beg: the reversal

sizzling with drama and music

that means *you were right*
all along. That's why you

keep watching—like everyone else
holding their sodas in the dark.

She could be a friend,
a nice person who deserves

some goddam *justice*. You
can tell she'd like another life:

without so many
hard decisions coming down

to only one. Maybe

you really are the character
other people think you are,

even though they can't hear
what's playing in your head.

After the movie, you walk
back into the mall wondering

if you could do what
she did. *That was*

pretty good, you mutter
with no one nearby

and light all over your face.

RIDDLE 3

for Philando Castile

The heart is about
the size of a fist.
The heart knows

this knows it
holds a hard place
that sings

to the blood
the way a long street
carries a whisper

from a high window
late at night. Revenge
is like this: like

a song with no
song in it—
the heart clenched

like a fist, rage
painting a room
in the blood's house:

the color
hard to resist
like the question

why?—like love,
like memory, like two
holes in the chest:

blood oiling the seat.
Witness: a son—a father

murdered, disappeared.
There is

so much sadness
in living

with what cannot
be undone. The heart

knows loss
is part of it: knows

the blood wants
a different story:

what hate has taken
love will replace

with a fist
ready to sing.

THE DOLLARS

"I'm all in!"

Do they own you?
Do they
make you
do whatever
they want? Do they

own you? Do you
work and pay and
work? Are you
nervous?

Is it hard
to sleep? Do they
gotchu? Was it
hard to wake
up?

What about your *hair?*
Does it keep
happening? Are you
doing your
best?
Do you need
a little
something?

Are you dressed?
Are you getting dressed?
Are you almost dressed?
What about
your hair?

Are you tired? Are you
hard to wake up?
What time is it?
How about
now? Do they
need more? Do they
make you? Did they
make you

over? Are you half-
dressed? Do they
own you? Do you
think
what you're
supposed to? Are you
saving? Who
are you

saving? Are you

tired? Are they
watching? Is it
hard?
Do you *ever*
wake up?
Do they
own
you? Do you
wake up

when they
want you to? Are they
everywhere? Are you
on
time?

How about now?
How about

now? Do you
do *the work?* Did you do
the do? Did they
do you?

Are you trying
to get
dressed?
Are you? Did you?
Will you?

Do they
own you?
Do they *still*
own you?

DU-DU BLUES VILLANELLE

Bad days happen for no reason at all
Feel like I'm down in a deep du-du pit
Maybe I've lived my whole life like a doll

Went to the Men's Room—got stuck in a stall
Guess my whole life I been lost in some shit
Looks like I was born for no reason at all

Remember bein little and tryin'a be tall?
Broke *G.I.Joe*—and just about flipped
Pop said, *Don't spend all your time witta doll*

Headed for the rally, but stopped in the mall
Ain't it always easy to just buy some shit?
Clerk gave me the side-eye for no reason at all

Wanna be Jesus, but my heart's pretty small
I'd like to see white people dancin for tips
History scoffs   for no reason at all

Half the time, felt like a house made'a straw
Spend most'a my days just a little bit pissed
I gotta stop walkin around like a doll

Been fightin the power, but *who you gonna call?*
Prolly be better to spend time wit'chur hips
Let's rock the night for no reason at all

Feel like bustin loose, but don't have the gall
Not sure what I mean, but you get my drift

Lived my whole life like a goddam doll
Ended up in the dookie for no reason at all

WITH *NAUGHTY BY NATURE*

hammering the headphones
and brass knuckles
icing its right fist,

the poem glares
from the library window.
Guard your grill, it spits,

watching the hurried drivers
held at the light. Many
had fallen under the spell
of The Lost Toupée—

his fetish for golden hair,
his faith in *alternative*
facts: fat blisters

on the face of an already
bubonic nation. The poem
had seen this shit
before, had grown sick

of saying itself—waiting
for somebody
to open a goddam book!

Rain spatters the street
but the sun is out.
And you know what that *means,*
the poem blurts,

I might have to
tune somebody up, tap-tap
that chin bone, maybe

knock a muthafucka out!
"Shhh," the librarian scolds,
index finger splitting
his skinny lips. The poem

turns around
slowly: *Guard your grill,*

it whispers, brass knuckles
bombastic in the bookish blight.

INVASION OF THE BODY SNATCHERS

"I'll be voting for Trump no matter what."

We only opened
our doors

when
we had to. We

shut our windows
but the smell

kept getting
worse, as if

someplace nearby
the carcass of an ape

was burning. Still
it seemed like

we were waiting
for someone.

It had gotten
late

but we
kept changing

our clothes.
All we really wanted

was a little sleep
before Monday

put us
back to work

but we *had*
been asleep—while

the new neighbors
were moving in
and

when we finally
did

fall awake,
we

saw them:
somehow looking

exactly like
us

waving from our
windows

wearing everything
in our closets,

honking by
in our cars

while we stood
in the street

touching our
faces.

LUCKY

After the mass killing at Pulse Nightclub in Orlando, Florida.

> *Rain falls into the open eyes of the dead*
> *again again with its pointless sound*
> --W.S. Merwin

Once: I thought I knew
how to read these words,
but I have fooled myself—
afraid to look at this
bad dream, this blind lobby,
this thanatocracy that
runs my country.

I am still astonished
by a certain calculated
ignorance—
despite all the grief
and all the *marches*:
the idea that brown skin
is reason enough
to stop a life.

So, it remains
hard to be black
here—and, of course, hard
to be female or poor
or queer—whatever
your complexion.

How long
before we know
each execution,
each exit wound
prints the blood
on all of us—

each of us often
alone   hoping
to dance with someone
who, for a moment, sees
only the promise of music
in our faces.

This morning, fresh light
opened your eyes
and told you
that *this* is what
eyes do: show the world

no matter how much
we don't want to see
how bad news breaks in,
breaks a day that seemed
like other days: a Monday
when you ran errands
slightly annoyed
by the price of bread.

Then, the TV voices:

adding up the dead,
"sorry for conflicting
reports," wondering
what the ____________ community
is feeling   *given such*
terror, given such a
terrible hing, given
this systemic insanity
loaded and delivered
as if by secret courier.

I have been close
to some killing,
not much. When that shooter
held the bell tower in Texas,
I was a kid in a city up north,
where boys like me
joined gangs to bleed
each other   and now

this in Florida, *this*—with me,
all grown up in Virginia
and a year ago, nine
black folks shot in their church
by some sick-fuck supremacist,
and yesterday another brother
murdered by a badge

in Minnesota, Louisiana, Illinois—
this is not *bad news*: this
is America
lighting your whole day
with death:
and you might believe
that you're blessed
not to have been *there*,

not to be a photograph
taped to a wall, not to "know

any
of the people
who died,"

but that's what
I mean, that's what I'm

trying to talk about: this daze,
this near intoxication, this

feeling *lucky*

that the blood on TV
isn't yours, that you're

alright—again,
that it isn't
you   again

who's dying

IT'S BEEN SOME TIME

for Primus St. John

since I could say something

that didn't further prove
my inability to change things

with a poem, but I think
I still believe in poetry:

a few words humming
like a lovelorn barbershop quartet

whose harmony makes me
wish the world could

sound like that,

despite the war in Gaza
and the almost-ready-to-be-active

shooters mumbling in my country,
despite so many people

trying to reach an itch
that won't be scratched—

and with a similar longing,
the sun squeezes

between these fat clouds
and I keep doing *this*

because I've been helped
by words

unsanctioned and sometimes impolite:
words borrowed from a language

lashed into our mouths
before we knew

what we were saying.
It's hard to understand

the history of the tongue:
its graceful generosity

in love, such outrageous agility
in speech, how it mostly

keeps to itself and doesn't
seem to mind

when we eat too much
or say something stupid

or hateful as we stumble around
inside our heads, consumed

by all we feel
and knowing—

though we
try not to know—

that what we really know
is impossible to say.

SEEKING ASYLUM,

the poem crosses the border—
without any state-approved
ID, with nothing that says
where it belongs. The wait
had become unbearable, so
much so that, when
the official asks, "Why
did you

leave your country,"
the poem turns
its palms up and sags
until two uniforms shove it
down the hall, out the door,
face first onto the bustling
lunchtime street

where the downtown hubbub
is punctuated by homeless
citizens, some screaming
to disprove their invisibility,
some curled like commas
on the sidewalk. A wind
pats down the trees:
heavy clouds have come
uninvited. *Maybe I can't belong*

anywhere,
the poem whispers. *Maybe*
I shoulda said
I had to leave 'cause
there's nowhere left to go, though
the poem—who'd spent its life
waiting to be understood—knows
that doesn't make any sense.

Being itself a stranger
estranged, the poem has
some niggling questions
about its own true
origins and its voice—which
usually goes unheard. *But Who Really*
Gives A Shit?! the poem shouts
as the back-to-work walkers
veer and scatter.

In some store windows
the poem almost sees its face:
brown, indelible, familiar,
disappearing quietly
like the mist that had just
begun to fall.

RUNAWAY BLUES VILLANELLE

Maybe we could all just fly away
Time will say nothing, but I told you so
Not sure what else time can really say

Not sure I wanna write this anyway
Woke up feelin like   I just don' know
Maybe we could all just walk away

No use runnin hot and yellin all damn day
Mom told me *No one monkey stops the show*
Guess she didn't know what else to say

Maybe I should put my mind on layaway
Can't turn it off—can't tell where it'll go
Think I might just turn away

Summa y'all go to church and pray
I look at the sky—   I just don' know
Maybe we should all just run away

Gotta try somethin to get outta the fray
If that don't work, they'll shrug *I told you so*
Ain't that some worthless shit to say?

People worry 'bout who's straight, who's gay:
The body's the arrow, the heart's the bow
Someday we'll all just fly away

When I go, just let Omar Sosa play
Then *rock'a my soul* at a *Funkadelic* show

You give me half a chance, I'd get away
When you think about it, same thing time would say

ACT IV

LIKE IT OR NOT,

the poem is growing
 older—and though fatigue
comes sooner these days,
the poem finds it almost
impossible to sleep. In fact,

Sleep walks past
the poem's house like
Angela Bassett
in red leather slacks,
like Cameron
Diaz   whose mouth

makes the poem wonder
how such lips might
flavor every word, but
the poem's inappropriate
thoughts are *not*

the problem. Sleep—
which slides by the poem
like a pickpocket, which
pecks the poem's cheek
briefly like a bird's shadow
on a bright day—is.

Some afternoons with Sleep
setting far off in the west, the poem
thinks about dying, that last

thumbs-downs and shrug,
but other than another scrim
dimming the view; other
than a grim tightening

in its chest, other than that
craven urge to shriek and sob
on the cold cobblestone
streets, the poem remains,
by all appearances, unaffected—

seems, in fact, coolishly
prepared to speak
as always: with a smile
that believes sanity

and compassionate
social transformation

are on the way—
that the poem itself

is *proof*   though

the poem worries
that this might

not at all be true,
that it may,

in truth, be drowning
rather than waving:

so, after tracing the dark
half the night,

the poem lights up

the TV: people
playing all the parts

convinced   and in
convincing ways.

"...NOTHIN UP MY SLEEVE"

--Bullwinkle

When you die
you cannot know

you're dead   and no one
tries to tell you either.

A small tree
of memories rustles

in your head, while
a Motown song just wheezes.

The last thing you remember
is a doctor shrugging off the cure.

You feel for the light switch
but only find that token

doorless door. The quiet grows

like a kind of brightness—
and the sound that sounds

is not a sound, unless
you count the sun

that never rises. Sadder still:
you're not alone

but there ain't no way
to prove it—just like now

above the ground, you're lonely
and there's no one

to undo it.

NOT BITTER BLUES VILLANELLE

Feel like I'm swimming but can't find the shore
Got up with the sun   but *up* ain't the same
Not sure I've ever been this way before

Thought I was drowning but not anymore
Got down with the backbeat and feel no strain
Mostly I'm swimming, just can't see the shore

Not feelin that feeble—just lost my allure
It's hard to be certain: maybe age is to blame
Anybody ever walked this way before?

Ever want groceries but can't find the store?
Maybe need somethin to clobber the pain?
Could be you've fallen but can't find the floor

Not really bitter, but my heart's pretty sore
So many things wash over my brain
I swam out too far and can't make the shore

Could be I'm falling but can't reach the floor
And maybe ain't no sense in tryin'a change
Simon says, "You never done like this before"

Right now, you know: you *don't* know the score
Just look at your shirt and add up the stains
You can tell you never been this way before

Why try to deny it? —I'm'a reach for the door
Gonna get me a ticket, catch that evenin train

Feel like I'm falling but can't reach the floor
But could be I'm swimming, just can't see the shore

POEM AT 64

for Michael Ryan

Always surprised to be
the age I am, though I guess
everything since puberty, I remember—
that first wet dream, leaving home
for college, *Shaft In Africa,*
scooping ice cream at Swenson's—

and I am by now, by all appearances,
someone who has *succeeded* somehow,
while a few good friends and early loves
have left this life, passed away,
"gone on," like my dad would quip
and shrug. What to do about so much

vanishing: the lazy grin you won't see
jump to a laugh, that voicemail
you cannot answer—
and finding your own jolly self
in line for departure, not wanting
to go but traipsing to the exit

anyway—like drifting toward the door
near the end of a party: chatting
with her and him, hugging some,
squeezing hands, and then,
you're completely outside:
streetlights and shadowy trees

walking you to the car. It just
doesn't matter maybe, maybe
it just   doesn't matter—
what we think
about death—that grief
is harder than anything

anyone can do. My father,
with his love for Count Basie
and lumpy buttermilk, is now
ashes. He has *gone on,*
joined *The Chapter Invisible*
as his Kappa brothers would say.

I remember him at 64:
forking sardines from those flat cans,
some nights pretending to be Redd Foxx,
then trudging up the stairs like
any other unfamous man. This was
twenty-five years before he found himself

staring down *The Rifleman*
on TV, almost nonchalantly waiting
for his diaper change. No one ever
imagines—I can't imagine
ever   struggling with a fork, hoping
someone will come to feed me.

My mother, slow-strolling the
Alzheimer's Road, still doesn't know
she's a widow. One time
she asked about "that man
who used to be here" the way
you'd inquire about a friend

not seen since high school
or an ice cream shop
closed long ago. I'm not mad

at anybody. Got nobody
to blame   though a bad
feeling keeps pushing me

around   like Big Sid used to
back in seventh grade.
Today I'm 64: born

sixty-four years ago,
today. And I might be here again
next year, but right now—

if I could make the time
and make myself less afraid—

I would cry like a baby
for everyone.

ANYMORE

for Phil Brady

Days when daylight
carries a touch
of night: the trees
late green with summer
whisper *autumn*
as though the coming
season were already here

and I guess we have
reached the age
where loss makes a way
into every conversation—
friends, teachers
dead and gone—as if
calling it out

as if naming death
and its daily thievery
might somehow
make it stay away.

I'm almost
a child again:
The boogeyman
only comes
when you turn off
the light

but even with my TV
burning all night
I don't sleep
so well anymore.

It's like being caught
with the wrong thing on
for winter and nothing
else to wear. For a while

I believed it was
the right-wing sickness
that had infected
my country.
For a while

I thought it was
just me   getting
older: my parents
recently gone, taking
their kindness with them.

Now I understand
it's been like this
all along: the snap and trill
of someone talking,
the tap of their good shoes
on the stairs

then silence—
with those of us left
unable to close our eyes,
trying to find the hours
where they still
might live.

MY MOTHER: MAY 1, 2020 / 5:36PM

This is what I remember:

Between her two last breaths
a long hesitation—

as if she thought she'd
heard something and paused

hoping it might be repeated
or maybe she finally realized

what she'd wanted to say all
along   and was not dying

just holding out for the words
so she could explain

something funny and unfortunate
and absolutely true

like on the phone with Auntie Margie
years ago: the story of a friend's

hard kiss that cracked a man's
front tooth. "Yes indeedy," she'd say

after a long, eye-watering laugh—
Yes indeedy.

———

Earlier, close to noon,
her eyes had opened

and she seemed to see
what we did not   but managed

only a noise, an inflection
probably older than this hovering

shadow called language. I admit
I *did* think she had always

and only been *my mother*—so
it's true, I did not know her

as well as I like to pretend
which doesn't make me

much more than just a little
lost   like most of us when we

really think about our mothers:

how they lived, who they were
before we came along.

———

She didn't open her eyes again
or acknowledge in any way

that you and I were sitting there
afraid, not knowing when the last

would come—as if death itself
were traveling slow backroads

from far away. Hard to tell
if she could still hear us

or if our hands on her arm
were comfort or nuisance

or if she had already set out
for a much quieter place

where remembering exactly
and trying to explain

doesn't matter at all.

AMUSEMENT PARK

Shuffling along, shouldering softly through the crowd,
you don't remember the admission or planning

to come. The rides look new, but it's mostly
the paint. Every day the sun disappears

and reappears   as if unsure of the situation.
Your parents used to talk about being

"young once." Now, you wonder what they
really wanted to say. Shadows

scratch the sidewalk. Popcorn, hotdogs,
pizza: aromas stoke the breeze.

Of course, fear takes the air too—
like the kind of perfume you only notice

when it's gone. You told your friends
"I'm sick of this shit," but somehow,

here you are   back in line,
itching for the *Wicked Flea*, a ride

famous for jumping the tracks, but
the whole park is like that. Even

the cross-eyed calico creeps
low to the ground as if ready

for some bad surprise. Worrying
this way, the cat is a lot like

the people who come here
to undo their daily lives: built

on hard work and
scary news—and bigotry

which usually moves around disguised
as someone else. Wherever you turn,

women, men: almost every hue, some skin
so dark it holds a hint of stars, other faces

white as paper, cinnamon-gold, or cocoa
with a kiss of brass. Of course, the fear

is shared unevenly—with all these colors
and the history they recall—but the people

remain lovely, enticing—a smorgasbord, ready
to be consumed   and, though strangers

exchange harmless glances, each
suspects the rest of playing a part

in a story that seems impossible
to explain—like the park itself:

both natural and not, both
deadly and full of fun.

The *Crazy Crook* is the scariest: *guaranteed*
to untie your mind the neon winks. Some get on

with glee, some with stolid faith, but you go
half-doubting, half-hoping it'll be alright

like your parents said   though lately, you haven't
seen them on any rides. Its height is legendary,

the loop-de-loops, ridiculous: that long, first climb,
the haphazard twists and dives, the whoops,

the shrieks and every time somebody yelling,
"Look, ma, no hands!" Maybe

the loudmouth is a superhero
ready to show off the courage

that makes Death and his shiny badge
back off—or maybe he's just another

dumb chump begging to be noticed
in a world that repaints and forgets,

refuels and drives on.
"Sit your simple ass down!" you snap,

while the *Crazy Crook* rolls over those bone-
bending swerves that snatch the riders

back to their bizzy, befuddled, stampeded lives:
out of hand and harder, faster—

as if some cranked up kidnapper has everyone
locked in his trunk and won't stop

stomping the gas: the days blur, each month
honks by like a V of Canada geese—you

spin around: your friends keep testing their
new knees. How did you get used

to this? When did you forget
how to sleep? What

made your parents
play certain words over

and over—*job, success,*
love, responsibility—and where,

exactly where did they go?

THE SUN SHONE

like most days in May and
some senators stopped
to watch the smoke thicken
and twist in the unsteady wind.

A few pointed, others half-
smiled as if unsure exactly
how to feel. Even though
it was on fire, the poem

sat stone still in the street.
Even with the acrid smell,
even as the poem's face turned
to ash and fell away

most thought this was just
one more trick, a well-played trope
setting up the poem to make
another impossible comeback:

raising its fist—traffic be damned,
baring its breast, saying what
poems usually say about war,
about sex, about the way this country

packs its maw with black
bodies, but the poem, sitting
in the lotus, did not blink
or move or seem to notice

the unhappy cars, the well-fed
White House lawn
or the curious tourists

aiming their phones for a selfie—
haze in their hair, heat wrinkling
the light behind them. The poem

didn't say *why*   it turned to fire
for its final word. Maybe it was just
sick of all these years getting up

getting dressed, tuning its throat
only to find itself disappeared
in America: Jabba the Hutt,
Commander in Chief.

There's only so much a poem can do
alone, before it's just talking
to itself   about talking to itself.

Why not fire?

Why not make *Meet The Press*
pay attention—just one day
of good blue suits asking

Who does that poem think it is?

But the poem doesn't think
about *who* it is. The poem doesn't
think anything. This is me talking—

me watching, while the poem burns.

HOW COULD YOU BLUES VILLANELLE

We fall for this life again and again
First light folds like a fleece on the cars
Did you ever think it never could end?

Though the chance for getting it right seems thin
And the news of our days runs cruel and bizarre
We fall for this life again and again

I often wonder about the ways of men—
The lies, the guns, the cries of guitar—
But I never thought it ever should end

If the kiss be kind, then show me the sin
I'll open my shirt and show you the scar
And beg for this life again and again

It's hard to hear myself over the din
I guess getting older has gone too far
But can you believe it's beginning to end?

I close my eyes when I look for a friend
And key the soft hum that comes from my car
Then pull into life again and again

Sidestep the storm in your head with a grin—
We bloody the Earth while it circles a star
Who even *thinks* it ever could end?

Hate to admit that I'm rounding the bend
Tapping my glass in the dust on the bar

Could you ever believe this ever would end?
Last call for this life   again and again

THIS PLACE

for Natalie Fish

No matter how many times
I've told myself *it'll be alright,*
no matter this breeze brushing the lake
or how much the late sun
paints the water, there are sorrows
we bear   only by bending
under their heft.

I'm thinking about your father
Big Jim: the easy glee in his smile,
his helpful hands, those faithful
blue suspenders, and the way
the phrase *I love you*
took his mouth by surprise
like a second language
he had to work to remember.

Of course, those words
were much too much and
nowhere near enough
for all that trundles
an old man's listing heart,
but when *you* said it,
he tried to say it back.

Those three sounds
must still mean something,
shopworn as they are—
just as this breeze remains
beautiful   despite everywhere
it's been. As daylight thins

in this place   and night
begins to point out the stars,

it's hard not to wonder
where he is now, where they go

when they're gone—and if
the love we tried to give

somehow stays with them
the way the warmth of a day

holds the grass
a good while after dark.

"WATCH ME PULL A RABBIT OUTTA MY HAT"

--Bullwinkle

When you die,
you do not know

you're done—and no one
runs to tell you either.

A single buttercup
sidles from your head

while the rush of Time
just freezes.

You remember being
on a bus,

then some bad news
about the weather.

You feel your forehead
for a bruise

but that worry
drifts untethered.

The silence shifts
and softs a sound—

it's like a change
of season. The Dark

lets down Her starlit hair
and loves you

for no reason.

ABOUT THE AUTHOR

Tim Seibles was born in Philadelphia in 1955. He was the Poet Laureate of Virginia from 2016 to 2018. His poems engage many aspects of life, from the romantic to the sociopolitical to the mystical. He is a former National Endowment for the Arts fellow and Provincetown Fine Arts Work Center fellow.

His eight books include *Hurdy-Gurdy, Hammerlock, Buffalo Head Solos,* and *Fast Animal,* a finalist for the 2012 National Book Award, winner of the Theodore Roethke Memorial Poetry Prize, and the Pen Oakland Josephine Miles Award for Poetry. *One Turn Around the Sun,* an extensive examination of his immediate family, was published in 2017.

In the last year, Tim has also written poems for two monuments. One in Norfolk, dedicated to the *Norfolk 17* who began the fearful process of integrating Virginia public schools, the other for an installation in Dallas, Texas, that addresses the many race-based lynchings that took place there.

His poems have appeared in several anthologies. Among them: *In Search of Color Everywhere, Seriously Funny, Uncommon Core, This is The Honey,* and *Villanelles.* Seibles' works have also been featured in *Best American Poetry* 2010, 2013, and 2023. His latest collection, *Voodoo Libretto: New & Selected Poems* was released by Etruscan Press in 2020.

BOOKS FROM ETRUSCAN PRESS

Zarathustra Must Die | Dorian Alexander
The Disappearance of Seth | Kazim Ali
The Last Orgasm | Nin Andrews
Son of a Bird | Nin Andrews
Drift Ice | Jennifer Atkinson
Crow Man | Tom Bailey
Coronology | Claire Bateman
Viscera | Felice Belle
Reading the Signs and other itinerant essays | Stephen Benz
Topographies | Stephen Benz
What We Ask of Flesh | Remica L. Bingham
The Greatest Jewish-American Lover in Hungarian History | Michael Blumenthal
No Hurry | Michael Blumenthal
Choir of the Wells | Bruce Bond
Cinder | Bruce Bond
The Other Sky | Bruce Bond and Aron Wiesenfeld
Peal | Bruce Bond
Scar | Bruce Bond
Until We Talk | Darrell Bourque and Bill Gingles
Big Time | Rus Bradburd
Poems and Their Making: A Conversation | Moderated by Philip Brady
Crave: Sojourn of a Hungry Soul | Laurie Jean Cannady
Toucans in the Arctic | Scott Coffel
Sixteen | Auguste Corteau
Don't Mind Me | Brian Coughlan
Wattle & daub | Brian Coughlan
Body of a Dancer | Renée E. D'Aoust
Generations: Lullaby with Incendiary Device, The Nazi Patrol, and How It Is That We |
Dante Di Stefano, William Heyen, and H. L. Hix

Ill Angels | Dante Di Stefano
Aard-vark to Axolotl: Pictures From my Grandfather's Dictionary | Karen Donovan
Trio: Planet Parable, Run: A Verse-History of Victoria Woodhull, and Endless Body | Karen Donovan, Diane Raptosh, and Daneen Wardrop
Scything Grace | Sean Thomas Dougherty
Areas of Fog | Will Dowd
Romer | Robert Eastwood
Wait for God to Notice| Sari Fordham
Bon Courage: Essays on Inheritance, Citizenship, and a Creative Life| Ru Freeman
Surrendering Oz | Bonnie Friedman
Funeral Playlist | Sarah Gorham
Nahoonkara | Peter Grandbois
Triptych: The Three-Legged World, In Time, and Orpheus & Echo | Peter Grandbois, James McCorkle, and Robert Miltner
The Candle: Poems of Our 20th Century Holocausts | William Heyen
The Confessions of Doc Williams & Other Poems | William Heyen
The Football Corporations | William Heyen
A Poetics of Hiroshima | William Heyen
September 11, 2001: American Writers Respond | Edited by William Heyen
Shoah Train | William Heyen
American Anger: An Evidentiary | H. L. Hix
As Easy As Lying | H. L. Hix
As Much As, If Not More Than | H. L. Hix
Chromatic | H. L. Hix
Demonstrategy: Poetry, For and Against | H. L. Hix
First Fire, Then Birds | H. L. Hix
God Bless | H. L. Hix
I'm Here to Learn to Dream in Your Language | H. L. Hix
Incident Light | H. L. Hix
Legible Heavens | H. L. Hix
Lines of Inquiry | H. L. Hix
Rain Inscription | H. L. Hix

Shadows of Houses | H. L. Hix
Wild and Whirling Words: A Poetic Conversation | Moderated by H. L. Hix
All the Difference | Patricia Horvath
Art Into Life | Frederick R. Karl
Free Concert: New and Selected Poems | Milton Kessler
Who's Afraid of Helen of Troy: An Essay on Love | David Lazar
Black Metamorphoses | Shanta Lee
Sign & Breath: Voice & the Literary Tradition | Edited by Shanta Lee and Philip Brady
Mailer's Last Days: New and Selected Remembrances of a Life in Literature |
J. Michael Lennon
Parallel Lives | Michael Lind
The Burning House | Paul Lisicky
Museum of Stones | Lynn Lurie
Quick Kills | Lynn Lurie
Synergos | Roberto Manzano
The Gambler's Nephew | Jack Matthews
American Mother | Colum McCann with Diane Foley
The Subtle Bodies | James McCorkle
An Archaeology of Yearning | Bruce Mills
Arcadia Road: A Trilogy | Thorpe Moeckel
Venison | Thorpe Moeckel
So Late, So Soon | Carol Moldaw
The Widening | Carol Moldaw
Clay and Star: Selected Poems of Liliana Ursu | Translated by Mihaela Moscaliuc
Cannot Stay: Essays on Travel | Kevin Oderman
White Vespa | Kevin Oderman
Also Dark | Angelique Palmer
Fates: The Medea Notebooks, Starfish Wash-Up, and overflow of an unknown self |
Ann Pedone, Katherine Soniat, and D. M. Spitzer
The Dog Looks Happy Upside Down | Meg Pokrass
Mr. Either/Or | Aaron Poochigian

Mr. Either/Or: All the Rage| Aaron Poochigian
Help Wanted: Female | Sara Pritchard
The Future of an Illusion | Rush Rankin
American Amnesiac | Diane Raptosh
Dear Z: The Zygote Epistles | Diane Raptosh
Human Directional | Diane Raptosh
I Eric America | Diane Raptosh
50 Miles | Sheryl St. Germain
Saint Joe's Passion | J.D. Schraffenberger
Lies Will Take You Somewhere | Sheila Schwartz
Fast Animal | Tim Seibles
One Turn Around the Sun | Tim Seibles
Voodoo Libretto: New and Selected Poems | Tim Seibles
Rough Ground | Alix Anne Shaw
The Blue Bridge | Maurya Simon
A Heaven Wrought of Iron: Poems From the Odyssey | D. M. Spitzer
American Fugue | Alexis Stamatis
Variations in the Key of K | Alex Stein
The Casanova Chronicles | Myrna Stone
Luz Bones | Myrna Stone
In the Cemetery of the Orange Trees | Jeff Talarigo
The White Horse: A Colombian Journey | Diane Thiel
The Arsonist's Song Has Nothing to Do With Fire | Allison Titus
Bestiality of the Involved | Spring Ulmer
The Waw | Jacqueline Gay Walley
Silk Road | Daneen Wardrop
Sinnerman | Michael Waters
The Fugitive Self | John Wheatcroft
YOU. | Joseph P. Wood
Leaves Borrowed from Human Flesh | Abigail Ardelle Zammit

Etruscan Press Is Proud of Support Received From

Wilkes University

Ohio Arts Council

The Stephen & Jeryl Oristaglio Foundation

Community of Literary Magazines and Presses

National Endowment for the Arts

Drs. Barbara Brothers & Gratia Murphy Endowment

Founded in 2001 with a generous grant from the Oristaglio Foundation, Etruscan Press is a nonprofit cooperative of poets and writers working to produce and promote books that nurture the dialogue among genres, achieve a distinctive voice, and reshape the literary and cultural histories of which we are a part.

etruscan press
www.etruscanpress.org
Etruscan Press books may be ordered from

US/Canada: Consortium Book Sales and Distribution
800.283.3572
www.cbsd.com

UK/Europe: Script Books
Tel: +44 (0)1226 734350
Email: orders@scriptps.co.uk

Etruscan Press is a 501(c)(3) nonprofit organization.
Contributions to Etruscan Press are tax deductible
as allowed under applicable law.
For more information, a prospectus,
or to order one of our titles,
contact us at books@etruscanpress.org.

www.ingramcontent.com/pod-product-compliance
Lightning Source LLC
Jackson TN
JSHW021222140526
102245JS00007B/2

* 9 7 9 8 9 9 0 7 6 7 8 4 3 *